I am a
Penguin

Karen Durrie

MEDIA ENHANCED BOOKS
AV2 BY WEIGL
ADDED VALUE • AUDIO VISUAL

www.av2books.com

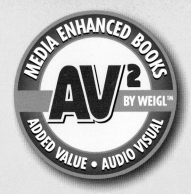

AV²
MEDIA ENHANCED BOOKS
BY WEIGL™
ADDED VALUE • AUDIO VISUAL

Go to **www.av2books.com**, and enter this book's unique code.

BOOK CODE

R622508

AV² by Weigl brings you media enhanced books that support active learning.

AV² provides enriched content that supplements and complements this book. Weigl's AV² books strive to create inspired learning and engage young minds in a total learning experience.

Your AV² Media Enhanced books come alive with...

Audio
Listen to sections of the book read aloud.

Key Words
Study vocabulary, and complete a matching word activity.

Video
Watch informative video clips.

Quizzes
Test your knowledge.

Embedded Weblinks
Gain additional information for research.

Slide Show
View images and captions, and prepare a presentation.

Try This!
Complete activities and hands-on experiments.

... and much, much more!

Published by AV² by Weigl
350 5ᵗʰ Avenue, 59ᵗʰ Floor New York, NY 10118
Website: www.av2books.com   www.weigl.com

Library of Congress Cataloging-in-Publication Data

Durrie, Karen.
 I am a penguin / Karen Durrie. -- 1st ed.
    p. cm. -- (I am)
 ISBN 978-1-61913-229-0 (hardcover : alk. paper) -- ISBN 978-1-61913-230-6 (softcover : alk. paper)
 1. Penguins--Juvenile literature. I. Title.
 QL696.S473D87 2013
 598.47--dc23

                                2011042349

Printed in the United States of America in North Mankato, Minnesota
1 2 3 4 5 6 7 8 9 0 16 15 14 13 12

012012
WEP060112

3 5944 00124 3599

Project Coordinator: Karen Durrie Art Director: Terry Paulhus

Weigl acknowledges Getty Images as the primary image supplier for this title.

I am a Penguin

In this book, I will teach you about

- myself
- my food
- my home
- my family

and much more!

I am a penguin.

4

I am a bird that swims but does not fly.

I keep my feathers dry with oil from my tail.

9

I can see very well under water.

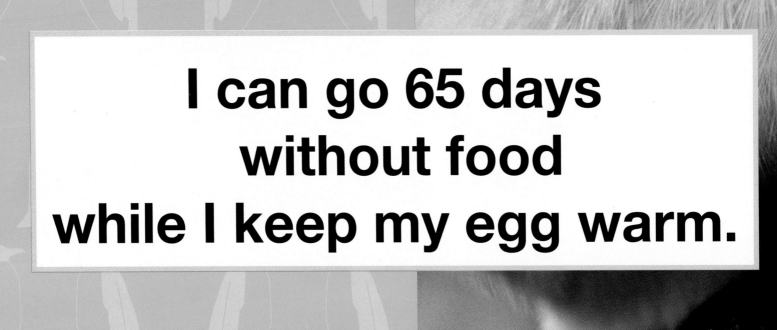

I can go 65 days
without food
while I keep my egg warm.

13

I have a call
that only my mother
and father know.

I have spikes
on my tongue.
They help me hold food.

17

I can swallow a fish in one bite.

I live by the ocean on ice or on land.

I am a penguin.

PENGUIN FACTS

These pages provide detailed information that expands on the interesting facts found in the book. They are intended to be used by adults as a learning support to help young readers round out their knowledge of each amazing animal featured in the I Am series.

Pages 4–5

I am a penguin. There are 17 types of penguin, all living in the Southern Hemisphere. The Emperor penguin is the largest, at about 4 feet (1.2 meters) tall, weighing 90 pounds (41 kilograms). The smallest is the fairy penguin, which stands less then 10 inches (25.4 centimeters) tall and weighs 2 pounds (0.9 kg).

Pages 6–7

Penguins are birds that swim but do not fly. Penguins have heavier skeletons than flying birds, and they have powerful flippers instead of wings. They are excellent divers and swimmers. Penguins can reach speeds of 15 miles (24 kilometers) per hour in the water.

Pages 8–9

Penguins keep their feathers dry with oil from their tail. Penguins use their bills to spread oil from a gland near their tails. When they preen their feathers, they spread the oil all over their bodies. The oil helps keep them warm and waterproof.

Pages 10–11

Penguins see clearly underwater. Penguins catch their food in the sea. They can see just as well underwater as on land. They can spot prey even in cloudy water. Penguins also have a third, clear eyelid that helps keep their eyes safe.

Pages 12–13

I can go 65 days without food while I keep my egg warm.

Penguins may go 65 days without food to keep their eggs warm. Male emperor penguins stop eating for about 65 days as they keep their mate's egg warm. The egg rests on his feet and is kept warm by his belly. Other penguins may also go more than 50 days without eating. Fat stores give them energy to survive.

Pages 14–15

I have a call that only my mother and father know.

Penguin chicks make a call only their mother and father know. Penguin chicks look alike, but adult penguins recognize and will feed only their chick. They know which chick is theirs because they learn its call when it is born. Penguins also know which mate is theirs by its call.

Pages 16–17

I have spikes on my tongue. They help me hold food.

Penguins have spikes on their tongues to help them hold their food. The food that penguins eat is slippery. They catch fish, shrimp, squid, krill, and octopuses. The penguin's spiky tongue helps it hold onto its prey.

Pages 18–19

I can swallow a fish in one bite.

Penguins can swallow a fish in one bite. Penguins do not have teeth. They have very sharp beaks and strong jaws. Penguins feed their chicks by spitting food they have eaten back up and into their chick's mouth.

Pages 20–21

I live by the ocean on ice or on land.

I am a penguin.

Penguins live by the ocean on ice or on land. Some penguins live in cold climates, and others live in tropical places. Some penguin populations are in decline. The African penguin population has decreased by 60 percent in the last 28 years. Threats to habitat, fishing, and pollution affect penguin numbers.

2/2013 P 598.47 20
Dur

WORD LIST

Research has shown that as much as 65 percent of all written material published in English is made up of 300 words. These 300 words cannot be taught using pictures or learned by sounding them out. They must be recognized by sight. This book contains 38 common sight words to help young readers improve their reading fluency and comprehension. This book also teaches young readers several important content words, such as nouns. These words are paired with pictures to aid in learning and improve understanding.

Page	Sight Words First Appearance	Page	Content Words First Appearance
4	a, am, I	4	penguin
6	but, does, not, that	6	bird
8	from, keep, my, with	8	feathers, oil, tail
10	can, see, under, very, water, well	12	egg
12	days, food, go, while, without	16	spikes, tongue
14	and, call, father, have, know, mother, only	18	fish
18	one	20	ice, ocean
16	help, me, on, they		
20	by, land, live, or, the		

24